The
CROSSINGS
GUIDE
to
OREGON'S COASTAL SPANS

Judy Fleagle

To Quinn —
This book was
great fun to put
together. I hope you
enjoy it!
Judy
Feb 1, 2013

Pacific Publishing
Florence • Oregon

Copyright © 2012 by Judy Fleagle

Printed in the United States of America

Photo credits on page 47

Cover photos, book design and composition by Robert Serra / Pacific Publishing

Library of Congress Control Number: 2012954234

ISBN: 9780985180119

Distributed by Pacific Publishing
P.O. Box 2767
327 Laurel Street
Florence, OR 97439
(541) 997-1040
www.connectflorence.com

First Edition

The
CROSSINGS
GUIDE
to
OREGON'S COASTAL SPANS

JUDY FLEAGLE

PACIFIC PUBLISHING • FLORENCE • OREGON

Bridge Locations

North Coast
1. Astoria-Megler Bridge — MP 4.1
2. Wilson River Bridge — MP 64.7

North Central Coast
3. Depoe Bay Bridge — MP 127.6
4. Rocky Creek Bridge — MP 130.0
5. Spencer Creek Bridge — MP 134.1
6. Yaquina Bay Bridge — MP 141.7
7. Alsea Bay Bridge — MP 155.5

South Central Coast
8. Cooks Chasm Bridge — MP 167.0
9. Cummins Creek Bridge — MP 168.4
10. Ten Mile Creek Bridge — MP 171.4
11. Big Creek Bridge — MP 175.0
12. Cape Creek Bridge — MP 178.4
13. Siuslaw River Bridge — MP 191.0

South Coast
14. Umpqua River Bridge — MP 211.1
15. Haynes Inlet Slough Bridge — MP 232.8
16. McCullough Memorial Bridge — MP 234.0
17. Brush Creek Bridge — MP 306.2
18. I.L. Patterson Bridge — MP 327.6
19. Thomas Creek Bridge — MP 347.9

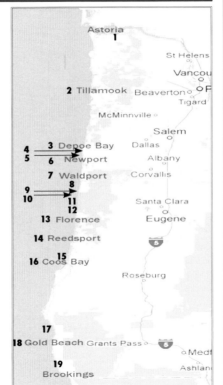

Contents

THE PACIFIC COAST HIGHWAY, also known as Highway 101, extends from the tip of Baja California in Mexico to the Olympic Peninsula in Washington. This includes the entire 363-mile length of the state of Oregon from the Columbia River to the California state line. Highway 101 through Oregon is not only a National Scenic Byway, but one of a select few highways designated as an All American Road. This is due to views of or access to the ocean all along the way.

This incredible highway is noted for its spectacular scenery, its beautiful lighthouses, its charming towns, and the historic bridges that tie it all together.

The Crossings Guide to Oregon's Coastal Spans covers 15 of those historic bridges from north to south and ends with a mention of four new spans that demonstrate a return to elegance in state bridge building. Of the historic bridges, a dozen were designed by Conde B. McCullough, one of the world's greatest bridge designers and Oregon State Bridge Engineer from 1919 through 1935 and Assistant State Highway Engineer until his death in 1946. The Guide also covers three historic bridges, built decades after McCullough's time, which still had ties to or were influenced by him. And it ends on a high note with the four new spans that look like they could've been designed by McCullough.

Once you've learned about these bridges, it will be hard to simply drive across or through them. You'll begin to appreciate them for their form as well as function and that is the purpose of this Guide.

The McCullough dozen—When driving through a McCullough bridge, look for concrete arches and aesthetic embellishments. Classic examples are decorated entry pylons and support piers—often in Art Deco style. Two of the largest bridges (Yaquina Bay and McCullough Memorial) also have elaborately decorated stairways at both ends.

If all you see when driving over a McCullough bridge are the railings, look underneath. If you can't get a good view from the road, pull over and check this Guide to see how you can get a good view of what's under the road deck.

McCullough built bridges that were efficient, economical, and elegant, and it's the elegant that made him stand out. The dozen he designed between 1927 and 1935 continue to be elegant, which is why visitors still take thousands of photos of them each year.

The other three—These non-McCullough bridges, built since his death in 1946, need to be included because of their importance: the Astoria–Megler Bridge (1966—Oregon's longest bridge), the new Alsea Bay Bridge (1991—built to replace the original 1936 McCullough bridge), and

continued on page 8

Trees along the river bank frame the Siuslaw River Bridge that connects the town of Florence to Glenada along the central coast.

the Thomas Creek Bridge (1961—Oregon's highest bridge).

World class collection of bridges easily accessible—These 15 bridges constitute one of the world's greatest collections of historic bridges and, all but the three newer ones, were designed by one of the world's greatest bridge designers. Fourteen are part of Hwy 101, and the 15th, the Rocky Creek Bridge, is on a bypassed section only one tenth of a mile off the present highway.

Zinc cathodic protection—To ensure that the dozen older bridges, built between 1927 and 1936, won't have to be replaced any time soon, a process called impressed current zinc cathodic protection is the answer. In this process, the concrete sections of a bridge are thoroughly restored before a coating of zinc is applied. Then electricity is run continu-

Oregon Department of Transportation Photo

ously through the reinforced steel within the concrete. The steel acts as the negative and the zinc as the positive, which means that the zinc draws the corrosion away from the steel and is sacrificed over time. Because the bridges must be totally renovated before applying the zinc, the process is complex and very time consuming, but it works. As of 2011, nine of the dozen bridges had undergone the process, including

CONDE B. MCCULLOUGH — One of the world's greatest bridge designers and Oregon State Bridge Engineer.

the southern section of the McCullough Memorial Bridge. The northern section will be next, followed by the Siuslaw River Bridge. The Umpqua River Bridge will be last. With the application of this process, this amazing collection of bridges will be around for decades to come. 🔄

The bluish gray color is
a result of the zinc coating on the Cummins
Creek Bridge.
JUDY FLEAGLE PHOTO

Astoria–Megler Bridge

Astoria–Megler Bridge (crosses Columbia River)—This extremely long bridge spanning the mighty Columbia was called the bridge to nowhere when it was built because folks thought no one would use it. That has not been the case. As of 2008, the daily traffic was 6,800 vehicles. The Astoria–Megler Bridge is 4 miles long and at the time it was built was considered the longest continuous three-span through-truss bridge in the world. When it was completed in 1966, it not only connected Oregon and Washington but completed Hwy 101 as an unbroken link.

It has three distinct sections—the impressive elevated portion that corkscrews 360 degrees countercockwise as it rises nearly 200 feet over Astoria into the 2,468-foot steel cantilever through truss, the 2-mile viaduct that is only about 25 feet above the water, and the elevated seven steel through truss spans on the Washington side. With its three totally different designs, it looks like it was put together by committee. However, it did have a designer—William A. Bugee, the Washington State Bridge Engineer. The man in charge of actually building the bridge was Ivan D. Merchant from the Oregon State Highway Department, and that's the McCullough connection. Merchant was hired by McCullough in 1929 and worked with him for years in the bridge section. I'm sure some of McCullough's ideas and innovations were used on the bridge, but the design wouldn't have passed muster. McCullough always took the whole structure into consideration, trying for a distinctive but coherent look.

This bridge is technically not located on the coast and neither is Astoria. Both are actually 14 miles upriver, but ask anybody in Oregon and they'll tell you that, of course, Astoria's on the coast.

This very long bridge was built with an amazingly strong foundation. The piers sit as far as 85 feet below the water level with piling supporting them. The piling extend down as far as 190 feet below the river bottom. This bridge was built to withstand a current of 9 mph, wind speeds up to 150 mph, and flood debris, including whole trees, ramming into it. So far, it's withstood everything that Northwest winters could throw at it and should be around long into the future.

Note: Once a year the Astoria–Megler Bridge closes to vehicular traffic and opens to pedestrians during the Great Columbia Crossing 10k, usually held in October. All participants are shuttled to the Washington side and can run, walk, or push a stroller to the Oregon side. Registration closes when a capacity of 3,000 participants is reached.

The four-mile-long
Astoria–Megler Bridge
crosses the Columbia
to Washington.
ROBERT L. POTTS PHOTO

This bridge section was barged down river from where it was fabricated.
OREGON DEPARTMENT OF TRANSPORTATION PHOTO

The approach corkscrews around and up over Astoria on its way across the Columbia River. OREGON DEPARTMENT OF TRANSPORTATION PHOTO

Wilson River Bridge (Tillamook)—This small span in Tillamook, along with Big Creek and Ten Mile Creek bridges (between Florence and Yachats) also built in 1931, were among McCullough's most challenging bridges. Don't let the small size and simplicity fool you. The 100-foot wide channel had no solid rock on the sides with which to anchor supports. This prevented McCullough from using traditional arches that required large sturdy abutments (end supports) to counter lateral thrust (pushing out).

Note: Also called the "Historic Bridge" by locals, the Wilson River Bridge is named for an early settler who brought the first cows into the Tillamook Valley. The bridge is located within a stone's throw of the parking lot of the Tillamook Cheese Factory.

To solve the problem, McCullough designed a 180-foot bridge with a 120-foot, reinforced-concrete tied arch. A tied arch practically holds itself up, requiring less sturdy abutments on either end. This bridge plus the two built between Yachats and Florence were the first bridges of this type built in the Northwest. After the construction of these small spans, McCullough incorporated the tied arch design in many of his larger spans.

In a tied arch, the outward-directed horizontal forces that try to flatten the arch are redirected and become compression arches, squeezing the ends together and are connected by the road deck or tie rods. It sounds complicated, but just picture a bow with the string stretched between. This makes one integrated—and stronger—structure. Hence the alternate name "bowstring" arch.

Because of this innovative arch design, McCullough made the list of top bridge designers in 1999 when *ENR* (formerly *Engineering News-Record*) celebrated its 125th anniversary by publishing a list of the top people who had made outstanding contributions to the construction industry since 1874.

Oregon Department of Transportation Photo

The original cross bracings had an X shape.

Notice the detail work
and the straightened
overhead bracing.
CHUCK CONNELL PHOTO

Depoe Bay Bridge

Depoe Bay Bridge—This McCullough bridge in the town of Depoe Bay bears the distinction of being his first reinforced-concrete arch coastal bridge. It has a deck arch design, which means you have to look below. Although it's called the Depoe Bay Bridge, it's actually two bridges side by side—each 312 feet long. The original was built in 1927 and the slightly wider western side was added in 1940. On the northern end, a sidewalk underpass makes it possible to walk under the road deck to the other side. This is a great opportunity to see how closely the two sides match.

The bridge was widened because the 18-foot roadway did

Note: The Depoe Bay Bridge spans what is called the world's smallest navigable harbor, and the bay is home to several resident gray whales each summer.

not include sidewalks. In 1927 there was no town, but by 1940, Depoe Bay had grown into quite a fishing village and needed pedestrian sidewalks on the bridge. The road deck wasn't reconfigured into four lanes until years later.

Oregon Department of Transportation Photo

By 1940, the bridge needed to be widened to provide sidewalks.

The Depoe Bay Bridge
is actually two bridges.
OREGON DEPARTMENT OF
TRANSPORTATION PHOTO

Rocky Creek (Ben Jones) Bridge (between Depoe Bay and Newport)—This is another deck arch design built in 1927 and the only McCullough bridge that was originally on Hwy 101 but is no longer. The bridge didn't move; the highway did. It was redesigned wider and slightly farther east up over Cape Foulweather.

The bridge is only one tenth of a mile off the highway. The old road, now called Otter Crest Loop, is one of the few segments remaining of the original Oregon Coast Highway completed in 1932. It leads to the village of Otter Rock and is accessed just south of the Rocky Creek State Scenic Viewpoint.

The turnoff is most easily approached from the north. From the south turn into Rocky Creek SSV and immediately turn back south onto the old highway. Very shortly, within a few eye blinks, you'll cross the Rocky Creek Bridge.

Just like the Depoe Bay Bridge, the interesting part is below the road deck. This bridge is 360 feet long, and you have to turn into the interpretive wayside and look back to

Note: The wayside's interpretive panels explain the importance of McCullough, cathodic protection, and Ben Jones. The bridge was named to honor Jones, a state legislator from Lincoln County, who introduced legislation in 1919 to build the Oregon Coast Highway. He is known as the "Father of the Coast Highway."

Oregon Department of Transportation Photo

The unfinished bridge is quite close to the stormy ocean.

see the 160-foot deck arch below. This symmetrically designed bridge is very pleasing to the eye and a favorite of coastal bridge aficionados. When it started showing serious deterioration in the late 1980s, bridge maintenance crews became alarmed. This bridge is very close to the waves and the salt spray, which caused corrosion of the reinforcing steel and the resultant cracking and breaking off of chunks of concrete. In 2001, it received major restoration and cathodic protection to ensure decades of future use.

The Rocky Creek
Bridge is definitely
worth a brief side trip.
CHUCK CONNELL PHOTO

Yaquina Bay Bridge (Newport)—This large bridge that crosses Yaquina Bay is probably the most well-known bridge on the coast and definitely the most photographed. Its over-the-top 75th birthday celebration in 2011 involved a whole month of activities in Newport, culminating in a parade that included a band, cheerleaders, old cars, and almost 1,000 bridge aficionados crossing the bridge.

This is one of two of McCullough's large bridges that were built very close to the waves. The other one, the Alsea Bay Bridge, is no longer standing. This one still stands due to the restoration and cathodic protection completed in three different phases over a 10-year period on the reinforced concrete portions of the bridge and due to almost constant maintenance of the

Note: The two main piers supporting the central arch look the same above the water, and each extend 50 feet below the water surface, but they have very different foundations. The northern one is anchored into bedrock. And the southern pier is supported by wooden piling driven 40 feet or more below the river bottom—actually approximately 700 piling support that one pier. Hard to imagine!

The 600-foot central arch took two months for completion.

three main arches constructed of steel.

Every part of this bridge is worth checking out, especially the stairways. At each end of the bridge are two elaborately decorated stairways—one on each side—to the grassy areas below. You need to walk up one of these and at least part way across the bridge to really appreciate the decorative touches and the grandeur of the central arch. From any angle, the Yaquina Bay Bridge is a beauty.

Yaquina Bay Bridge:
The most photographed
span on the coast.
ROBERT SERRA PHOTO

Alsea Bay Bridge (Waldport)—For 55 years, vehicles crossed the original Alsea Bay Bridge built in 1936 and designed by McCullough. During that time, the reinforced concrete corroded from exposure to the salt air causing the concrete to crack and break off in chunks, and wooden piling that formed the bridge's foundation fell victim to marine worms.

The new Alsea Bay Bridge, begun in the summer of 1988, opened to traffic in the fall of 1991. After new bridge completion, the old bridge underwent demolition October 1, 1991.

The new bridge incorporated a reinforced-concrete structure with a steel arch, having a 450-foot span that rises an impressive 90 feet above the bridge deck. Even though made of steel, it's painted to blend in with the reinforced concrete.

The new Y-shaped bridge support piers have all the reinforcing steel coated with sealers to prevent salt intrusion. And the concrete around the reinforcing steel is four inches thick instead of an inch. The piling forming the foundation below the support piers are made of steel and concrete (not timber this time) and reach more than 100 feet—all the way to the bedrock below. With all of the state-of-the-art improvements, the new bridge should last at least 100 years.

Note: Construction of the new bridge involved adding a wayside north of the bridge where some of the decorative pylons from the original bridge are displayed and an interpretive center at the southern end, featuring exhibits about the original bridge and its designer—McCullough. The Historic Alsea Bay Bridge Interpretive Center is a must stop for bridge aficionados.

Oregon Department of Transportation Photo

The new Alsea Bay Bridge was dedicated in the fall of 1991.

The "new" Alsea Bay
Bridge celebrated its 20th
anniversary in 2011.
ROBERT SERRA PHOTO

Cummins Creek Bridge

Cummins Creek Bridge (between Yachats and Florence)—This small bridge built in 1931 and named after F.L. Cummins, an early homesteader in the area, gives no clue that it is of any importance. Once again, you have to look below the bridge to see a graceful deck arch that supports the road deck.

No side view is possible unless you drive into Neptune State Scenic Viewpoint (SSV). From the parking area, you can partially see the arch below the bridge. But if you walk a short distance down a trail, you get a grand view.

This is the only bridge designed by McCullough on Hwy 101 that is not listed on the National Register of Historic Places. Apparently, due to lack of documentation, there is speculation that this bridge, although usually attributed to McCullough, may not have been designed by him. And that's why it wasn't included.

The spandrel columns connecting the road deck and deck arch look similar to those on other McCullough deck arches, and the decorative flutings on the main piers, spandrel columns, and railings are typical McCullough as well as the brackets supporting the railings. So it certainly has the look of a McCullough-designed bridge.

Note: Lines scored into the concrete surface create the illusion that it's constructed of stone blocks, which is also seen on the I.L. Patterson Bridge, designed by McCullough, over the Rogue River. Both bridges were completed in 1931.

Oregon Department of Transportation Photo

The Cummins Creek Bridge was completed the year before the highway was completed.

The Cummins
Creek Bridge can
only be seen from
Neptune State Scenic
Viewpoint.
JUDY FLEAGLE PHOTO

Ten Mile Creek and Big Creek bridges (between Yachats and Florence)—These small tied arch bridges, located between Yachats and Florence, are almost identical to the Wilson River Bridge in Tillamook. As was previously mentioned, these three were the first bridges of this type in the Northwest when they were built in 1931. The tied arch McCullough designed for these sites represents his engineering ingenuity.

These two bridges, like the Wilson River Bridge in Tillamook, have no rocky embankments with which to anchor supports. But since the tied "bowstring" arch practically holds itself up, both bridges could be built without massive supports.

If you look at historic photos taken when these three bridges were built in 1936, each had X-shaped cross bracing. That is no longer the case. Today the X-shaped cross bar

Note: Pull over just north of the Ten Mile Creek Bridge on the west side of Hwy 101 and take a trail through the dune grass to where you can look back at the bridge. Do this early in the day to avoid wind. With no wind, you may get a photo with a reflection.

Oregon Department of Transportation Photo

Notice the cross bracing on the new Ten Mile Creek Bridge in 1931.

has been cut off at the middle of the X and straight bars have been extended to each side. It now makes the shape of a K. This is the case on each end of all three bridges.

McCullough bridges expert, Dr. Robert W. Hadlow, author of *Elegant Arches, Soaring Spans*, supplied this information regarding the redesign: "Within the past 10 to 15

continued on page 28

The Ten Mile Creek
Bridge is one of three
identical tied arch
bridges on the coast.
ROBERT SERRA PHOTO

Note: Because the Big Creek Bridge was in such bad condition, the state considered replacing it. According to Ray Allen in *Oregon Coast Bridges*, this is when the silverspot butterfly entered the picture. Allen explains that building a temporary bridge during construction of a new bridge would have infringed on critical butterfly habitat. Instead of becoming bogged down in an environmental battle, ODOT, the U.S. Fish & Wildlife Service, and the Federal Highway Administration agreed on a rehab plan for the bridge. And there were enough reserve funds to do the X braces retrofit on the Ten Mile Creek Bridge. So we can thank the endangered silverspot butterfly for continued use of these historic bridges.

years, ODOT retrofitted the portal bracing on the Wilson River, Ten Mile Creek, and Big Creek bridges because the original X formation provided low vertical clearance at the outside edge of the travel lanes."

The two bridges located so close to the ocean waves had received exten-

Much wood was used in the scaffolding and forms on the Big Creek Bridge.

sive corrosive damage over the years from the salt air requiring extensive repair of all concrete and metal structural components. After the X braces retrofit and repairs, both bridges received the impressed current zinc cathodic protection—Big Creek in 1998 and Ten Mile Creek in 2007.

Notice how the cross bracing in the Big Creek Bridge has been cut off to form a K shape.
JUDY FLEAGLE PHOTO

Cape Creek Bridge (between Yachats and Florence)—This bridge, completed in 1932 in the style of a Roman aqueduct, is the only bridge of this type in Oregon. Because of the steep, rugged headlands, this section of coast was the last completed during the construction of the Oregon Coast Highway. The old stagecoach road went over one headland, down to sea level, and back up over another headland in this area—very difficult for the automobiles of the time. So this bridge and the adjacent tunnel were constructed to straighten out the highs and lows.

It was not cheap: This section became known as "the million dollar mile." One inland editor complained about the expense in an editorial that read, "The state in its infinite wisdom is constructing a bridge more than 100 feet high over a creek that doesn't even come to my knees!" He was clearly annoyed, but those who drive this highway appreciate not having to go over the headlands.

If you turn off at Heceta Head Lighthouse State Scenic Viewpoint, it takes you to the best view of the bridge as well as the lighthouse. This is one of the most scenic locations on the entire Oregon coast.

Note: The Cape Creek Bridge was the first of the coast's historic reinforced concrete bridges to undergo total restoration and the impressed current zinc cathodic protection. In 1991, the headline read, "First Bridge to be Electrified in the World." When the coastal bridges were built, they were considered cutting edge—apparently, this one still is.

Siuslaw Pioneer Museum Photo

Notice the opening for the tunnel, the tiny bridge being replaced, and the arches taking shape.

The Cape Creek Bridge is
the only aqueduct-style
bridge in the state.
ROBERT SERRA PHOTO

Siuslaw River Bridge (crosses Siuslaw River at Florence)— This impressive bridge is noted for the four Egyptian obelisk style pier houses, reminiscent of castle turrets, that are located on each side of the double-bascule lift span. With the major renovations begun in 2009 that continued through 2010, this bridge looks the best it has looked since it was built in 1936.

Note: At less than half a mile across, it's a great walking bridge. By walking, you can see all the artistic embellishments up close and see how nice the bridge looks these days.

The Siuslaw River Bridge is considered by some to be the bridge that best represents McCullough's technical and aesthetic genius. That's why Judith Dupre, author of *Bridges: A History of the World's Most Famous and Important Spans*, included a large photo of this bridge to represent McCullough bridges.

It is not the largest or as well known as the Yaquina Bay Bridge in Newport or the McCullough Memorial Bridge over Coos Bay. But because it was built with such precision, because it is a double bascule drawbridge that opens to allow marine traffic, and because of all the artistic embellishments in Art Deco, Moderne, Gothic, and Egyptian styles, it is considered a technological and aesthetic jewel of a bridge.

The best views are from Bay Street in Florence's Old Town.

Oregon Department of Transportation Photo

Almost as much wood was used in scaffolding and forms as would have been to build a wooden bridge.

The Siuslaw River Bridge
is said to best represent
McCullough's technical
and aesthetic genius.
ROBERT SERRA PHOTO

Umpqua River Bridge

Umpqua River Bridge (Reedsport)—Before the bridge, a ferry ran from Gardiner to Reedsport—about 2 ½ miles.

Connecting the two towns by way of a highway involved crossing two rivers and an island. It was quite an undertaking. Bolon Island was swampy on the northern end and had a high ridge of solid rock along its southern edge. The original plans called for drilling a 550-foot tunnel through the ridge. That plan was scrapped, however, in favor of making one of the largest road cuts in the state up to that time.

Note: Turn west at the Dunes Headquarters and drive over the little hill to go under the bridge. Here you can look through the support arches to get a cathedral effect. It's quite lovely.

The ridge was 180 feet high and 140 feet of it had to go. A swath was cut through that was 600 feet long and 400 feet wide at the top with gradual slopes. Notice the giant road cut as you drive across Bolon Island.

Oregon Department of Transportation Photo

N. from Bunkers 10

The swing span opens to allow marine traffic along two corridors.

This bridge opens as a swing bridge to let marine traffic through. At 430 feet, the swing span designed by McCullough was the largest of its kind in Oregon. The bridge tender's house is high in the cross bracing and is only manned when the bridge is to be opened. Look up! It's still there. Today swing bridges are usually seen on railroads. This is the only one still operating on an Oregon highway. The best views of the bridge are from the boardwalk area fronting the river.

The Umpqua River Bridge
is the only swing-span
drawbridge left in the
Oregon highway system.
ROBERT SERRA PHOTO

McCullough Memorial Bridge (crosses Coos Bay to North Bend)—At a little more than a mile across, this bridge was the largest bridge built in Oregon at the time (1936) and still is. The Astoria–Megler Bridge is longer but ends up in Washington.

This bridge was built with a double cantilever design. A cantilevered bridge is built by projecting out from a supporting pier on one side while maintaining a counterbalance on the opposite side to keep the first side from tipping over into the bay. This meant that whatever was done on one side had to be done on the counterbalancing side or have supports in place, either temporary or permanent. And this whole process was repeated 793 feet away on the other side of the navigation channel. Building both cantilevers and then having them connect precisely in every way in the middle to complete the 1,708-foot

Oregon Department of Transportation Photo

The concrete arches and steel cantilever show how the bridge is taking shape.

Note: Of all the hundreds of bridges McCullough was involved with, this one spanning Coos Bay was his favorite. And in 1947, the year after he died, this bridge was renamed the Conde B. McCullough Memorial Bridge in his honor.

steel truss took endless careful planning. It was considered an engineering marvel at the time. Today driving through the Gothic arches of the steel truss section is mesmerizing and beautiful.

McCullough didn't skimp on the aesthetics. Three sets of stairways leading from the bridge down below are incredibly ornate—absolute works of art. Once down below, look through the arches to obtain the cathedral effect. This works best on the southern end of the bridge.

This mile-long bridge was
a marvel of engineering
when it was built.
ROBERT SERRA PHOTO

Isaac Lee Patterson Bridge (crosses Rogue River to Gold Beach)
—This bridge, named after Oregon's governor from 1927 through 1929, is the oldest of the large coastal spans designed by McCullough. It was built in 1931 and dedicated in 1932. Upon completion, it was the largest bridge between San Francisco and Astoria. With its seven deck arches below the road deck, you can't see them when you're crossing, but because of how this bridge is sited, whether approaching from north or south, you get a fabulous view.

By designing the I.L. Patterson Bridge, McCullough showed that he could design a large reinforced concrete bridge at the coast. The coast with its constant salt spray in the air rusts steel and rots wood, so reinforced concrete was McCullough's construction material of choice.

During construction, McCullough tried a new technique never before used in the United States. It was called the Freyssinet method, where through a complicated process, lighter, more graceful supports were possible due to the use of less concrete. McCullough wanted to see how it worked. He discovered that it worked just fine, but because it required more skilled labor, it didn't save money. So he never used it again. But he shared what he learned in a technical report, adding to the annals of bridge building. And in 1982, the I.L. Patterson Bridge was designated a National Historic Civil Engineering Landmark by the American Society of Civil Engineers because of McCullough's experimental use of the Freyssinet method.

Note: Since its four-year restoration completed in 2005, which included the zinc cathodic protection, it looks terrific. LED lights at night highlight its deck arches, making them especially lovely when there's a bit of fog.

Oregon Department of Transportation Photo

The pristine new bridge as seen from the north.

The bridge over the
Rogue River as seen
from the south.
OREGON DEPARTMENT OF
TRANSPORTATION PHOTO

Thomas Creek Bridge (9 miles north of Brookings)—This bridge's claim to fame is that it's the highest bridge in the state. Completed in 1961 many years after McCullough died, it still has a connection to him. It was designed by Ivan D. Merchant, the same engineer in charge of building the Astoria–Megler Bridge a few years later. This is the engineer McCullough hired in 1929 and worked with closely for years. Merchant designed this steel deck bridge supported by two steel towers that rise 345 feet from foundations set on either side of Thomas Creek. It's not a style reminiscent of McCullough, but the steel towers are similar to the ones supporting the steel truss section on the Astoria end of the Astoria–Megler Bridge.

Note: The second highest bridges in the state are the Crooked River High Bridge designed by McCullough (now open only to pedestrians) and the nearby newer Crooked River (red) Bridge completed in 2000. They are located near Terrebonne in Central Oregon and both are approximately 300 feet high—almost 50 feet shorter.

When the bridge was being built, it was constructed from the top down with cantilevered sections suspended out over the abyss supported by temporary towers of wood with narrow walkways having no railings. Safety nets were required and the workers wouldn't work without them—well most of the workers wouldn't. The Navajo iron workers refused to work with safety nets because they felt it brought bad luck. So a compromise was reached: The nets were taken down for the Navajos and rehung when their high steel work was completed. Then the concrete and carpentry deck crews could get back to work. A watchman had been hired to keep onlookers from the unprotected edges when there were no nets. And the watchman had to stay on after they were rehung because local teenagers started jumping off the bridge into the nets when the work crews weren't there!

The bridge was built to bypass the 37-mile ride from Cape Sebastian inland over Carpenter Hill and down into Brookings. The narrow, two-lane, windy mountain road simply became too dangerous as vehicles outgrew it—especially large RVs.

Because the Thomas Creek Bridge has no superstructure above the road deck, you barely know you're crossing a bridge. And it's hard to see very far below the bridge from either end because foliage has grown up.

continued on page 42

This aerial shot shows the whole 345-foot-high bridge, which is difficult to see from land.
ALEX DERR PHOTO

Oregon Department of Transportation Photo

There are two 0.5 mile trails that offer views of the bridge.* One starts on Hwy 101 at MP 348.2 and parallels the highway, swings around an open hillside, plunges through forest, traverses the head of a draw, and goes up toward the south Thomas Creek parking area. A side trail leads to a spot below the bridge for great photos.

The second trail leaves Hwy 101 at the northwest corner of the bridge. It goes through a wooded area, a grassy area, and back to Hwy 101 at North Islands Viewpoint. (Or just stop at the North Islands Viewpoint.) A side trip across the meadow to the knob west of the trail allows you to look back and see the bridge.

To truly appreciate the magnitude of the height of the Thomas Creek Bridge, park at one end and walk to the middle. Even with the railing, it's a dizzying sight. So be prepared to hang on tight.

This steel truss bridge has two very tall legs.

* Trail info is from *Oregon Coast Trail, Curry County, Hiking in the "Banana Belt"* by Walt Schroeder, MP 348.2 8). To Thomas Creek Bridge & 9). Thomas Creek Bridge to North Islands Viewpoint. (www.goldbeach.org/index.php/attractions/oregon-coast-trail)

THOMAS CR BRIDGE
HIGHEST BRIDGE IN OREGON
HEIGHT 345 FEET

101

While crossing, it's hard to
tell that this is the tallest
bridge in Oregon.
OREGON DEPARTMENT OF
TRANSPORTATION PHOTO

Four small unremarkable reinforced-concrete girder bridges have been replaced during the past dozen years with elegant new bridges. The replacements with their deck-arch designs are reminiscent of what McCullough might design. They are listed here from north to south:

The Spencer Creek Bridge (left) at Beverly Beach State Park north of Newport, completed in 2008, boasts a single sturdy arch composed of three massive ribs. This bridge is built to resist even large tsunamis and looks like it. Drive into the state park for the best view. Chuck Connell Photo

Cape Perpetua's Cooks Chasm Bridge's single arch, (right), which connects fairly high up on the bank on each end, was completed in 2003 and is best seen from the Chasm's viewing area. Judy Fleagle Photo

Haynes Inlet Slough Bridge (above) was built in two phases: The east side was completed in 2001 and the west side in 2004. The end result is a five-lane bridge supported by three graceful arches. It is located just north of Coos Bay. Brush Creek Bridge (right) is located near Humbug Mountain State Park between Port Orford and Gold Beach. It was completed in 2000 and boasts a single arch with a slightly modern look. Both of these bridges were built with cutting edge technology and should last 120 years.

Oregon Department of Transportation Photos

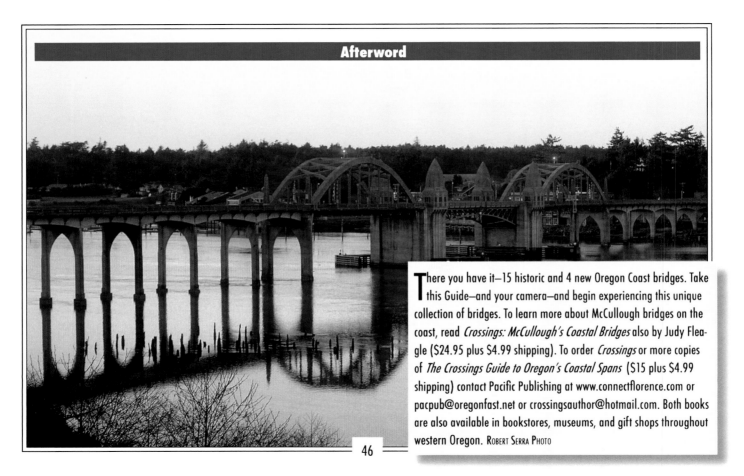

There you have it—15 historic and 4 new Oregon Coast bridges. Take this Guide—and your camera—and begin experiencing this unique collection of bridges. To learn more about McCullough bridges on the coast, read *Crossings: McCullough's Coastal Bridges* also by Judy Fleagle ($24.95 plus $4.99 shipping). To order *Crossings* or more copies of *The Crossings Guide to Oregon's Coastal Spans* ($15 plus $4.99 shipping) contact Pacific Publishing at www.connectflorence.com or pacpub@oregonfast.net or crossingsauthor@hotmail.com. Both books are also available in bookstores, museums, and gift shops throughout western Oregon. ROBERT SERRA PHOTO

Acknowledgments & Credits

Many thanks to the following . . .

Oregon Department of Transportation:
• Candice Stich for her encouragement and offering ODOT's help—Strategic Systems & Data Management Manager
• Robert W. Hadlow for information on the retrofit of the cross bracing on the Wilson River, Ten Mile Creek, and Big Creek bridges—Senior Historian
• Tom Ohren for locating and sending all the historic photos requested—Drafting, Graphics & Imaging
• Greg Westergaard (Photo/Video Unit) and Laura Wilt (Librarian) for sending the Haynes Inlet Slough Bridge photo

Photographers:
• Chuck Connell for trying again and again on the Wilson River Bridge and for photos of some north central coast bridges—Tillamook videographer
• Alex Derr for sending the perfect aerial photo of the Thomas Creek Bridge—Seal Rock photographer
• Robert L. Potts for sending so many beautiful shots of the Astoria–Megler Bridge that it was hard to decide—Astoria photographer
• Robert Serra for believing in this project and traveling the coast more than once to get just the right shot of several bridges—publisher and designer of this Guide and *Crossings: McCullough's Coastal Bridges*

Others:
• Ray A. Allen for information about the silverspot butterfly connection to the Big Creek and Ten Mile Creek bridges gleaned from his book—author *Oregon Coast Bridges*
• Sue Dawson for information on the I.L. Patterson and Thomas Creek bridges that no one else seemed to know—Gold Beach Visitor Center
• Fred Jensen for the Cape Creek Bridge historic photo—curator Siuslaw Pioneer Museum

Cover Photographs:
Robert Serra

Inside Photographs:
Theresa Baer—48
Chuck Connell—15, 19, 44
Alex Derr—41
Judy Fleagle—9, 25, 29, 44
Oregon Department of Transportation—8, 12, 13, 14, 16, 17, 18, 20, 22, 24, 26, 28, 32, 34, 36, 38, 39, 42, 43, 45
Robert L. Potts—11
Robert Serra—1, 2, 3, 7, 21, 23, 27, 31, 33, 35, 37, 46
Siuslaw Pioneer Museum—30

Judy Fleagle graduated with a major in Elementary Education and a minor in English. She made good use of them by spending 22 years teaching 1st and 2nd grades in Los Gatos, California, and, after moving to Florence on the Oregon coast, spending 21 years as an editor and staff writer for *Oregon Coast* and *Northwest Travel* magazines.

Fleagle often wrote about McCullough bridges in *Oregon Coast* and during the 2005 update of the magazine's annual *Mile by Mile Guide,* she inserted information about each of McCullough's coastal bridges after they were listed on the National Register of Historic Places. She has an abiding love for these bridges and a huge respect for McCullough. Since retiring as

an editor at the magazines, she continues as a freelance writer, editor, and author.

Her other books, *Crossings: McCullough's Coastal Bridges,* published in 2011, is in its third printing, and *Chuck and Jean: the Interesting Years,* was published in 1992 and dealt with her parents' remembrances.

Judy Fleagle at the
Siuslaw River Bridge
in Florence.
Theresa Baer Photo